200

CLASSIC
COCKTAILS

200

CLASSIC
COCKTAILS

TOM SODEN

An Hachette UK Company
www.hachette.co.uk

First published in Great Britain in 2016 by
Hamlyn, a division of Octopus Publishing Group
Carmelite House, 50 Victoria Embankment
London, EC4Y 0DZ
www.octopusbooks.co.uk
www.octopusbooksusa.com
Copyright © Octopus Publishing Group Ltd 2016

Distributed in the US by Hachette Book Group
1290 Avenue of the Americas
4th and 5th Floors, New York, NY 10020

Distributed in Canada by Canadian Manda Group
664 Annette St, Toronto, Ontario, Canada M6S 2C8

Tom Soden asserts the moral right to be identified as the
author of this work

ISBN 978-0-60063-223-8

Printed and bound in China

10 9 8 7 6 5 4 3 2 1

The measure used in the recipes is based on a bar jigger
of 1 oz, or 2 tablespoons (note that jiggers vary in size and
a pony may be available in 1 oz). If preferred, a different
volume can be used, providing the ratios are kept constant
within a drink and suitable adjustments are made to spoon
measurements, where they occur. Standard level kitchen
spoon and cup measurements are used in all recipes.
The U.S. Food and Drug Administration advises that eggs
should not be consumed raw. This book contains some
recipes made with raw eggs. It is prudent for vulnerable
people, such as pregnant and nursing mothers, people
with weakened immune systems, and the elderly
to avoid these recipes.
This book includes recipes made with nuts and nut
derivatives. It is advisable for those with known allergic
reactions to nuts and nut derivatives to avoid these recipes.
It is also prudent to check the labels of prepared ingredients
for the possible inclusion of nut derivatives.
The U.S. Department of Health and Human Services
recommends that men do not regularly exceed 2 drinks
a day and women 1 drink a day, a drink being defined as
0.5 oz of pure alcohol, the equivalent of 1.5 oz of 80-proof
distilled spirits. Those who regularly drink more than this run
an increasingly significant risk of illness and death from a
number of conditions. In addition, women who are pregnant
or trying to conceive should avoid drinking alcohol.

contents

introduction

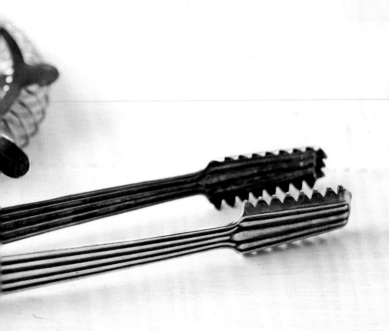

what makes a good cocktail?

Good cocktails, like good food, are based around the quality of the ingredients, and using them in the correct ratios. Jiggers vary in size, so the recipes in this book use measures. The measure used for the recipes is a 1 oz measure, but you can use a larger measure as long as you keep the ratios the same. For example, if you use a 1½ oz jigger, use 1½ tablespoons when 1 tablespoon is given. Don't forget: 1 oz = 2 tablespoons; 8 oz = 1 cup; and with liquor available in metric, 250 ml = about 1 cup.

Using fresh and homemade ingredients makes a big difference between a good drink and an outstanding drink. All ingredients can be found in grocery stores, kitchen stores, or online.

cocktail ingredients

ice

This is a key part of cocktails, and you'll need plenty of it. Purchase it from your supermarket or freeze big containers of water, then crack it up to use in your drinks. If you're hosting a big party and want to serve punches (see page 204), which will need a lot of ice, it may be worth finding a local ice supplier that supplies catering companies.

citrus juice

It's important to use fresh citrus juice in your drinks; it will have the best taste and produce the best drinks. Store your fruit out of the refrigerator at room temperature. Look for a soft-skinned fruit for juicing, which you can do with a juicer or citrus press. You can keep fresh citrus juice for a couple of days in the refrigerator, sealed to prevent oxidation.

sugar syrup

You can buy sugar syrup to make cocktails or you can make your own. The most basic form of sugar syrup is easy to make by mixing superfine sugar and hot water and stirring until the sugar dissolves. (You can process granulated sugar in a food processor to make superfine sugar.) The key when making sugar syrups is to use a 1:1 ratio of sugar to liquid.

basic sugar syrup

makes **4 cups** of sugar syrup

dissolve 5 cups **superfine sugar** in 4 cups of
  hot water.

Let cool. Sugar syrup will keep in a sterilized
bottle in the refrigerator for up to 2 weeks.

You can use different types of sugar to
make sugar syrup. White sugar acts as a flavor
enhancer, while dark sugars add toffeelike
flavors, which work well with dark liquors.

flavored syrups

You can buy flavored syrups or make your
own, using one of these three option.

The first is by adding a flavored extract to a
sugar syrup made on a 1:1 ratio as described
above. ForRose Syrup, for example, add
2 tablespoons rose extract to 5 cups superfine
sugar dissolved in 4 cups of hot water.

The second way to make a flavored syrup
is with a fruit-flavor tea. Make some strong
fruit-flavor tea and use it as the basis for your
sugar syrup, using equal measures of tea
and superfine sugar. For 4 cups of Lemon
& Ginger Syrup, for example, mix 4 cups
hot lemon & ginger tea with 5 cups white
superfine sugar and stir until dissolved. Make
sure you remove the tea bags prior to adding
the sugar or things will probably get messy!

Creating syrups from fresh fruit, herbs, or
spices is also easy. The basic recipe, which you
can vary, is as follows:

basic flavored syrup

makes **4 cups** ruit syrup

8 oz **fruit** or 3 tablespoons of **spices**
  (use the whole spice instead of powdered)

4 cups **water**

5 cups **white superfine sugar**

1 Remove any thick, inedible peel from the
fruit and remove any stems, pits, or seeds,
because they add a tannic flavor to your syrup.
2 Put the fruit or spices into a saucepan, add
the water, and bring the water to a rolling boil.
Lower the heat and simmer for 30 minutes,
topping up with water, if required, or until the
fruit is stripped of its color. Taste the water
to check how much of the flavor has leached
into it. Spices and fruit vary in how fast they
develop flavor.

3 Remove from the heat and strain into a heatproof bowl. Discard the fruit or spices. Mix the hot fruit or spice liquid with the sugar until dissolved.

4 Let cool, decant into a sterilized bottle, and store in the refrigerator until required.

to make raspberry & pineapple syrup
(see page 78), use the quantities listed below and follow the method above.

½ **large pineapple**, peeled and cubed

2 cups **raspberries** (the riper the better and don't be afraid to use blemished fruit)

4 cups **water**

5 cups **white superfine sugar**

to make spiced sugar syrup
(see page 216), use the quantities listed below and follow the method above.

3 **cinnamon sticks**

1 tablespoon **star anise**

2 **nutmegs**

1 teaspoon **cloves**

1 teaspoon **allspice**

4 cups **water**

4½ cups firmly packed **light brown sugar**

ginger juice

This adds a fiery, warming kick to cocktails and is healthy. Simply run peeled ginger through a juicer or, if no juicer is available, blend until smooth, then strain.

cucumber juice

Incredibly refreshing, 1 cucumber will make a small glass of juice. Simply run peeled cucumber through a juicer or, if no juicer is available, blend until smooth, then strain.

oleo-saccharum

This is a syrup produced from the oil of citrus zest and sugar. Superfine sugar dissolves best.

citrus fruit oleo-saccharum

citrus fruit

white superfine sugar (allow 2 tablespoons sugar per large lemon, 3 tablespoons per orange, and ¼ cup per grapefruit)

1 Wash the fruit. Use a vegetable peeler to peel the zest from the fruit, removing as little white pith as possible. Put the zest into a small bowl.

2 Add the sugar and press the sugar and zest firmly with a muddler, pestle, or wooden spoon until the zest begins to express oils.
3 Let the mixture sit at room temperature for an hour, until the sugar has dissolved.

shrubs

A shrub is an acidic fruit syrup that combines sugar, fruit, and vinegar. Apple cider vinegars work best, but you could use many different fruit and rice vinegars.

This recipe can be adapted for various shrubs.

orange & fennel seed shrub

4 oranges

1 tablespoon **fennel seeds**

1¼ cups **superfine sugar**

1 cup **apple cider vinegar**

1 Wash and peel the oranges. Cut the oranges into quarters. Lightly crush the fennel seeds.
2 Put the orange quarters, orange peel, and crushed fennel seeds into a bowl, mix together, and lightly press with a muddler, pestle, or wooden spoon to release some of the juices.
3 Cover the mixture with the sugar. Mix thoroughly, cover, and place in the refrigerator for 24 hours. The fruit should be surrounded by a syrup.
4 Remove from the refrigerator and lightly press again to remove any additional juices.
5 Strain the liquid into a clean bowl and scrape any remaining sugar into the bowl. Discard the fruit.

6 Add the vinegar to the liquid, then whisk until any remaining sugar is dissolved.
7 Pour into a sterilized bottle and keep in the refrigerator until required.

To make camomile & fennel seed shrub (see page 42), muddle 2 tablespoons crushed fennel seeds and the zest of 1 lemon with pith removed, in the bottom of a glass measuring cup to release the citrus oils. Add 1 cup each of apple cider vinegar and rice vinegar and 3 camomile tea bags. Steep for 4–5 hours. Strain the liquid, then add 2½ cups white superfine sugar until dissolved. Pour into sterilized bottle and refrigerate until required.

infused liquors

Infusing your own liquors with fruit and spices is fun and easy. To infuse a liquor, remove any inedible skins, stems, or seeds from your chosen fruit and add the fruit to the liquor. Most fruit can sit in the liquor indefinitely, but some spices need to be removed before they impart too strong a flavor. Below are recommended fruit or spice volumes along with steeping times. To infuse, put the liquor and fruit or spices into a large, sterilized sealable jar and let sit in a warm, dark place, such as a kitchen cabinet. The warmth will assist in the maceration. Shake the jar each day to mix the infusion.

almond-infused rum (see page 52)
Add 1 cup **crushed almonds** to 3 cups (750 ml) **rum** and let infuse for 3–4 weeks.

apricot-infused vodka (see page 34)
Add 2 cups **dried apricots** to 2 cups (500 ml) **vodka** and let infuse for at least 5 days.

apricot & cinnamon-infused vodka
(see page 34)
Add 2 cups **dried apricots** and 2 **cinnamon sticks** to 2 cups (500 ml) **vodka** and let infuse for at least 5 days.

cinnamon & nutmeg-infused bourbon
(see page 108)
Add 2 **cinnamon sticks** and 1 **whole nutmeg** to 2 cups (500 ml) **bourbon** and let infuse for 5–7 days.

cucumber-infused gin, rum, or vodka
(see pages 30, 100, 206)
Add ½ medium **cucumber** to 2 cups (500 ml) **gin**, **white rum**, or **vodka** and let infuse for 24 hours.

ginger-infused cognac (see page 220)
Add 2 cups peeled and sliced **fresh ginger root** to 2 cups (500 ml) **Cognac** and let infuse for 2–3 days.

ginger & green cardamom-infused gin
(see page 208)
Add 1 cup peeled and sliced **fresh ginger root** and 1 teaspoon **green cardamom pods** to 2 cups (500 ml) and let infuse for 2 days.

mango-infused gin (see page 106)
Add 1 medium **mango**, peeled, pitted, and chopped, to 3 cups (750 ml) **gin** and let infuse for at least 3 days.

mint-infused vodka (see page 224)
Add 5–6 sprigs of **mint** to 2 cups (500 ml) **vodka** and let infuse for 24 hours.

pineapple-infused campari (see page 112)
Add ⅓ large **pineapple**, peeled and cubed, to 3 cups (750 ml) **Campari** and let infuse for at least 3 days.

pineapple & cherry-infused rum
(see page 212)
Add ¼ large **pineapple**, peeled and cubed, and 1 tablespoon **maraschino cherries** to 2 cups (500 ml) **white rum** and let infuse for at least 5 days.

raspberry-infused aperol (see page 210)
Add 2 cups **raspberries** to 2 cups (500 ml) **Aperol** and let infuse for 7–10 days.

star anise-infused vodka (see page 150)
Add 2 tablespoons **star anise** to 2 cups (500 ml) **vodka** and let infuse for 3–5 days.

orange & cherry-infused bourbon
(see page 40)
Muddle 6 slices **orange** and 6 **candied** cherries in a jar and add 2 cups (500 ml) **bourbon**. Let infuse for 24 hours and strain.

choosing glasses

There are thousands of different cocktails, but they all fall into one of three categories: long, short, or shot. Long drinks generally have more mixer than alcohol and are often served with ice and a straw. The terms "straight up" and "on the rocks" are synonymous with the short drink, which tends to be more about the liquor, which is often combined with a single mixer, at most. Finally, there is the shot. These miniature cocktails are made up mainly from liquor and liqueurs and are designed to give a quick hit of alcohol. Cocktail glasses are tailored to the type of drinks they will contain.

champagne flute
Used for champagne or champagne cocktails, the narrow mouth of the flute helps the drink to stay fizzy.

champagne saucer
These old-fashioned glasses are not practical for serving champagne, because the drink quickly loses its fizz.

margarita, or coupette, glass
When this type of glass is used for a margarita, the rim is dipped in salt. These glasses are used for daiquiris and other fruit-base cocktails.

martini glass
A martini glass, also known as a cocktail glass, is designed so that your hand can't warm the glass, making sure that the cocktail is served completely chilled.

highball glass
A highball glass is suitable for any long cocktail, from the Cuba Libre (see page 86) to Long Island Iced Tea (see page 82).

collins glass

This is similar to a highball glass but is slightly narrower.

wine glass

Sangria (see page 206) is often served in a wine glass, but they are not usually used for cocktails.

old-fashioned glass

Also known as a rocks glass, the old-fashioned glass is great for any drink that's served on the rocks or straight up. It's also good for muddled drinks.

shot glass

Shot glasses are often found in two sizes—for a single or double measure. They are ideal for a single mouthful, which can range from a Tequila Shot to the more decadent layered B-52.

brandy sniffer glass

These glasses are usually used for fine liquors, where aroma is as important as the taste. The glass can be warmed to encourage the release of the aroma.

hurricane glass

This type of glass is mostly found in beach bars, where it is used to serve creamy, rum-base drinks.

parfait glass

Often used by bartenders for mixing cocktails, the parfait glass is also good for fruity drinks.

Irish coffee glass

An Irish coffee glass is generally used for a hot drink, such as Irish Coffee.

cordial glass

This has a short stem and comes in a variety of shapes. It has a smaller bowl, making it useful for sweet liqueurs and brandies.

useful equipment

There are a few tools that are worth investing in if you are planning to make cocktails.

shaker
The Boston shaker is the most simple option, but it needs to be used in conjunction with a hawthorne strainer. Alternatively, you could choose a shaker with a built-in strainer.

measure, jigger, or pony
Single and double measures are are essential for mixing ingredients so that the proportions always are the same. Look for a jigger or pony with a 1 oz measure for recipes in the book.

mixing glass
A mixing glass is used for those drinks that require only a gentle stirring before they are poured or strained.

hawthorne strainer
This type of strainer is often used in conjunction with a Boston shaker, but a simple tea strainer will also work well.

bar spoon
Similar to a teaspoon but with a long handle, a bar spoon is used for stirring, layering, and muddling drinks.

muddling stick
Similar to a pestle, which will work just as well, a muddling stick, or muddler, is used to crush fruit or herbs in a glass or shaker for drinks, such as the Mojito (see page 116).

bottle opener
Choose a bottle opener with two attachments, one for metal-to bottles and a corkscrew for wine bottles.

pourers
A pourer is inserted into the top of a liquor bottle to enable the liquid to flow in a controlled manner.

food processor
A food processor or blender is useful for making frozen cocktails and smoothies.

the liquors and their partners

Each liquor has a natural affinity with certain flavors, and it is from these complementary relationships that cocktails are born.

brandy

Much brandy is distilled from grapes, but there are some varieties that use other fruits as their base. Serve brandy with fruit and fruit juices, but don't use the finest brandies for mixed drinks.

gin

A clear grain liquor infused with juniper berries, gin was first produced in Holland more than 400 years ago. Serve it with citrus fruits, fresh berries, and tonic water.

rum

This Caribbean staple, which dates back to the seventeenth century, is made from sugar cane leftovers after sugar production. Serve rum with any of the exotic fruits, cream, or cola.

vodka

Vodka is distilled from grain and is relatively free from natural flavor. There is fierce debate on its origins, with both the Poles and the Russians claiming to have invented the drink. With its neutral character, it is infinitely mixable with a huge range of flavors. Serve it with cranberry, tomato, or citrus juices, or for a classic drink simply add tonic water.

tequila

Mexico's best-known liquor is made from the blue agave plant, and its origins can be traced back to the Aztecs. It was traditionally served by itself as a Tequila Slammer, but also works well with citrus and sour fruits as well as ginger and tomato.

whiskey

The origins of whisky are hotly debated, with both Scotland and Ireland staking a claim to having developed it from fermented grain. Modern whiskies have a much smoother taste and texture, and can be blended or unblended. Serve it with water, club soda, or ginger ale.

17

perfecting your technique

With just a few basic techniques, your bartending skills will be complete. Follow the step-by-step instructions to hone your craft and mix perfect cocktails.

blending

Frozen cocktails and smoothies are blended with ice in a blender until they are of a smooth consistency. A frozen daiquiri or margarita is made using a virtually identical recipe to the unfrozen versions but with a scoop of crushed ice added to the blender before blending on high speed. Be careful not to add too much ice to the recipe, because it will dilute the cocktail. It's best to add a little at a time.

shaking

The best-known cocktail technique and probably the one that you use most often, so it's important to get right. Shaking is used to mix ingredients quickly and thoroughly, and to chill the drink before serving.

1 Fill a cocktail shaker halfway with ice cubes, or cracked or crushed ice.

2 If the recipe calls for a chilled glass, add a few ice cubes and some cold water to the glass, swirl it around, and discard.

3 Add the recipe ingredients to the shaker and shake until a frost forms on the outside. Use both hands, one at each end, so that it doesn't slip.

4 Strain the cocktail into the glass and serve.

muddling

Muddling is a technique that is used to bring out the flavors of herbs and fruit, using a blunt tool called a muddler, and the best-known muddled drink is the Mojito (see page 116).

1 Add mint leaves to a highball glass. Add some sugar syrup and some lime wedges.

2 Hold the glass firmly and use a muddler or pestle to press down. Twist and press to release the flavors.

3 Continue this for about 30 seconds, then top off the glass with crushed ice and add the remaining ingredients.

building

This is a straightforward technique that involves nothing more than putting the ingredients together in the correct order.

1 Have all the ingredients for the cocktail on hand. Chill the glass, if required.

2 Add each ingredient in recipe order, making sure that all measures are exact.

double-straining

When you want to prevent all traces of pureed fruit and ice fragments from entering the glass, use a shaker with a built-in strainer in conjunction with a hawthorne strainer. Alternatively, strain through a fine strainer.

layering

A number of liquors or liqueurs can be served layered on top of each other; because some are lighter than others, they float on top of your cocktail. One of the best-known layered drinks is the Grasshopper (see page 162).

1 Pour the first ingredient into a glass, being careful that it does not touch the sides.

2 Position a bar spoon in the center of the glass, rounded part down and facing you. Rest the spoon against the side of the glass as your pour the second ingredient down the spoon. It should float on top of the first liquid, creating a separate layer.

3 Repeat with the third ingredient, then carefully remove the spoon.

stirring

A cocktail is prepared by stirring when the ingredients need to be mixed and chilled, but it's important to maintain the clarity. This ensures that there is no fragmented ice and no air bubbles throughout the drink. Some stirred cocktails require the ingredients to be prepared in a mixing glass, then strained into the serving glass with a fine strainer.

1 Add the ingredients to a glass in the order stated in the recipe.

2 Use a bar spoon to stir the drink, lightly or vigorously, as described in the recipe.

3 Finish the drink with any garnish, if desired, and serve.

highballs
& collins

tom collins

makes **1**
glass **collins**
equipment **cocktail shaker,
  strainer**

2 measures **gin**
1 measure **sugar syrup**
1 measure **lemon juice**
ice cubes
4 measures **club soda**

To garnish
lemon wedge
black cherry

Put the gin, sugar syrup, and lemon juice into a cocktail shaker and fill with ice cubes.

Shake, then strain into a glass full of ice cubes and top up with the club soda. Garnish with a lemon wedge and a cherry and serve.

For a Ginty Collins, pour 2 measures gin into a collins glass and add 1 Earl Grey tea bag. Let steep for 1 minute before removing the tea bag. Fill the glass with ice cubes and add 1 measure lemon juice, 1 measure sugar syrup, 2 teaspoons grapefruit liqueur, and 2 dashes grapefruit bitters and stir gently. Garnish with a grapefruit twist and serve.

whisky highball

makes **1**
glass **collins**

ice cubes
2 measures **Scotch whisky**
1 dash **Angostura bitters**
4 measures **club soda**
lemon twist, to garnish

Add 3 large ice cubes and the whisky and Angostura bitters to a glass. Stir gently, then fill the glass with more ice cubes and top up with the club soda. Garnish with a lemon twist and serve.

For an Ichi Highball, add 4 cucumber slices, 1 measure umeshu, and 1½ measures Scotch whisky to a glass and press the cucumber with the end of a bar spoon to release some of the flavor. Fill a collins glass with ice cubes, then top with 4 measures club soda and stir. Garnish with a cucumber strip and serve.

berry collins

makes **2**
glasses **highball**
equipment **muddler**

8 **raspberries**, plus extra
    to garnish
8 **blueberries**, plus extra
    to garnish
1–2 dashes **strawberry syrup**
crushed ice
4 measures **gin**
4 teaspoons **lemon juice**
sugar syrup, to taste
club soda, to top up
lemon slices, to garnish

Muddle the berries and strawberry syrup in the bottom of each glass, then fill each glass with crushed ice.

Add the gin, lemon juice, and sugar syrup. Stir, then top up with the club soda. Garnish with berries and lemon slices and serve.

For a Lemon Grass Collins, divide 4 measures lemon grass vodka (see infused liquors, page 12) between 2 highball glasses full of crushed ice, then add ½ measure vanilla liqueur and 1 dash lemon juice to each. Add sugar syrup to taste and top up with ginger beer.

playa del mar

makes **2**
glasses **highball**
equipment **cocktail shaker,
  strainer**

2 **orange slices**
light brown sugar and
  sea salt, mixed
ice cubes
2½ measures **tequila gold**
1½ measures **Grand Marnier**
4 teaspoons **lime juice**
1½ measures **cranberry juice**
1½ measures **pineapple juice**

To garnish
pineapple wedges
orange zest spirals

Frost the rim of each glass by moistening it with an orange slice, then pressing it into the sugar and salt mixture.

Fill each glass with ice cubes. Pour the tequila, Grand Marnier, and fruit juices into a cocktail shaker. Fill the shaker with ice cubes and shake vigorously for 10 seconds, then strain into the glasses. Garnish each glass with a pineapple wedge and an orange zest spiral.

For a Sunburn, fill 2 highball glasses with ice, add 2 measures tequila gold, 1 tablespoon Cointreau, and 6 measures cranberry juice to each. Garnish with orange slices, if desired.

gin cucumber cooler

makes **1**

glass **collins**

equipment **muddler**

2 measures **gin**

5 **mint leaves**, plus an
  extra sprig to garnish

5 slices **cucumber**

3 measures **apple juice**

3 measures **club soda**

ice cubes

Add the gin, mint, and cucumber to a glass and gently muddle.

Let stand for a couple of minutes, then add the apple juice, club soda, and some ice cubes. Garnish with a sprig of mint and serve.

For an Eden's Club Collins, add 2 measures cucumber-infused gin (see page 12), 2 teaspoons elderflower liqueur, 5 mint leaves, 2 teaspoons lemon juice, and 2 measures apple juice to a cocktail shaker. Shake and strain into an ice-filled collins glass. Top up with 3 measures club soda, garnish with an apple slice or mint sprig, and serve.

sea breeze

makes **2**
glasses **highball**

ice cubes
2 measures **vodka**
4 measures **cranberry juice**
2 measures **grapefruit juice**
lime wedges, to garnish

Fill 2 highball glasses with ice cubes, pour the vodka, cranberry juice, and grapefruit juice over them, and stir well.

Garnish with lime wedges and serve.

For a Bay Breeze, replace the grapefruit juice with pineapple juice.

apricot collins

2 measures **apricot-infused**
  vodka (see page 12)
1 measure **lemon juice**
1 measure **sugar syrup**
ice cubes
4 measures **club soda**
apricot wedge, to garnish

Add the vodka, lemon juice, and sugar syrup to a cocktail shaker, then fill with ice cubes.

Shake and strain into a glass filled with ice cubes. Top up with the club soda, garnish with an apricot wedge, and serve.

For a Blossom Tree Fizz, add 2 measures apricot & cinnamon-infused vodka (see page 12), ½ teaspoon orange blossom water, 1 tablespoon sugar syrup, 4 teaspoons lemon juice, 1 measure orange juice, and 1 tablespoon egg white to a cocktail shaker. Whisk thoroughly, then add some ice cubes. Shake hard, then add 4 measures club soda and strain into an ice-filled collins glass. Garnish with grated orange zest and serve.

tijuana mary

makes **1**

glass **collins**

equipment **cocktail shaker, muddler, strainer**

4 chunks **watermelon**, plus extra to garnish

2 measures **tequila**

2 teaspoons **sriracha sauce**

1 pinch **salt**

2 pinches **pink peppercorns**

ice cubes

4 measures **tomato juice**

Put the watermelon chunks into a cocktail shaker and muddle. Add the tequila, sriracha sauce, salt, peppercorns, and some ice cubes and shake.

Strain into a glass full of ice cubes and top up with the tomato juice. Stir well, garnish with a watermelon wedge, and serve.

For a Summer Mary, add 2 measures vodka, 2 teaspoons lime juice, 1 measure orange juice, 2 teaspoons sweet chili sauce, 2 pinches celery salt, and 4 measures tomato juice to a collins glass. Top up with ice cubes. Score a celery stick to release its flavors, add to the glass, and serve.

Monte Carlo sling

makes **2**

glasses **highball**

equipment **muddling stick,**
   cocktail shaker, strainer,
   cocktail sticks

10 **seedless grapes**, plus
   extra to decorate

crushed **ice**

2 measures **brandy**

1 measure **peach liqueur**

2 measures **ruby port**

2 measures **lemon juice**

1 measure **orange juice**

2 dashes **orange bitters**

4 measures **Champagne**

Muddle 5 grapes in the base of each highball glass,
then fill the glass with crushed ice.

Put all the other ingredients, except the Champagne,
into a cocktail shaker and add more ice. Shake well and
strain into the glasses. Top up with the Champagne,
decorate with grapes and serve.

For a Fuzzy Navel, to serve 1, one of the easiest
cocktails to prepare, simply pour 1½ measures of peach
liqueur into a highball glass. Add plenty of ice and top
up with fresh orange juice.

bourbon mule

makes **1**
glass **collins**

ice cubes
2 measures **bourbon**
1 tablespoon **orange liqueur**
2 teaspoons **lemon juice**
4 measures **ginger beer**
2 dashes **Angostura bitters**
lemon and **lime wedge**,
  to garnish

Fill a glass with ice cubes, add the remaining ingredients, and stir.

Garnish with a lemon and a lime wedge and serve.

For a Cherry Buck Mule, fill a collins glass with ice cubes, add 2 measures orange & cherry-infused bourbon (see page 13), 4 teaspoons Triple Sec, 2 teaspoons lemon juice, and 2 teaspoons ginger juice, and stir. Top up with 4 measures club soda, garnish with a maraschino cherry or orange slice, and serve.

camomile collins

makes **1**
glass **collins**

2 measures **gin**
1 **camomile tea bag**
ice cubes
1 measure **lemon juice**
1 measure **sugar syrup**
4 measures **club soda**
ice cubes
lemon slice, to garnish

Pour the gin into a glass and add the tea bag. Stir the tea bag and gin together for about 5 minutes, until the gin is infused with camomile flavor. Remove the tea bag and fill the glass with ice cubes

Add the remaining ingredients, garnish with a lemon slice, and serve.

For an Orchard Collins, add 1 measure gin, 3 teaspoons lemon juice, 1 tablespoon camomile & fennel seed shrub (see page 11), and 1 measure apple juice to a cocktail shaker and shake. Strain into a collins glass filled with ice cubes and top up with 4 measures hard cider. Garnish with an apple slice and serve.

singapore sling

makes **2**
glasses **highball**
equipment **cocktail shaker,
   strainer**

ice cubes
2 measures **gin**
1 measure **cherry brandy**
½ measure **Cointreau**
½ measure **Bénédictine**
1 measure **grenadine**
1 measure **lime juice**
10 measures **pineapple juice**
1–2 dashes **Angostura bitters**

To garnish
pineapple wedges
maraschino cherries

Fill a cocktail shaker halfway with ice cubes and put some ice cubes into each highball glass. Add the remaining ingredients to the shaker and shake until a frost forms on the outside of the shaker.

Strain over the ice cubes into the glasses. Garnish each one with a pineapple wedge and a maraschino cherry and serve.

For a Gin Sling, shake the juice of 1 lemon, 2 measures cherry brandy, and 6 measures gin with plenty of ice. Strain into 2 highball glasses filled with ice and top up with club soda.

scotch ginger highball

makes **1**
glass **collins**

ice cubes
2 measures **Scotch whisky**
1 measure **lemon juice**
1 tablespoon **sugar syrup**
4 measures **ginger ale**
slice **fresh ginger root**,
  to garnish

Pour the whisky, lemon juice, sugar syrup, and ginger ale into a glass filled with ice cubes and stir.

Garnish with a slice of fresh ginger root and serve.

For a Highland Highball, add 2 measures Scotch whisky, 1 tablespoon citrus oleo-saccharum (see page 10), 2 teaspoons ginger juice, 2 teaspoons lemon juice, and 2 dashes Angostura bitters to a cocktail shaker and fill with ice. Strain into a collins glass filled with ice cubes, then top up with 4 measures club soda. Garnish with lemon wedge and crystallized ginger and serve.

los altos

makes **1**

glass **collins**

equipment **cocktail shaker, muddler, strainer**

5 slices **tangerine**

1 tablespoon **agave syrup**

2 measures **tequila**

2 teaspoons **lime** juice

2 teaspoons **Campari**

ice cubes

4 measures **club soda**

To garnish

orange slice

lime wedge

Add the tangerine slices and agave syrup to a cocktail shaker and muddle.

Pour in the tequila, lime juice, and Campari and shake. Strain into a glass filled with ice cubes and top up with the club soda. Garnish with an orange slice and a lime wedge and serve.

For a Paloma, pour 2 measures tequila, 3 measures white grapefruit juice, and 3 measures lemon-lime soda into a collins glass filled with ice cubes and stir. Garnish with a lime slice and serve.

apple jack ricky

makes **1**
glass **collins**
equipment **cocktail shaker,
strainer**

2 measures **apple brandy**
2 measures **pink grapefruit
juice**
2 teaspoons **sugar syrup**
ice cubes
4 measures **club soda**
pink grapefruit wedge,
to garnish

Add apple brandy, grapefruit juice, and sugar syrup to
a cocktail shaker.

Shake and strain into an ice-filled glass before topping
up with the club soda. Garnish with a pink grapefruit
wedge and serve.

For a Dusky Ricky, add 2 measures apple brandy,
4 teaspoons lemon juice, 1 tablespoon maple syrup,
1 measure orange juice, and 1 measure pink grapefruit
juice to a cocktail shaker and fill with ice cubes. Shake
and strain into an ice-filled collins glass. Top up with
2 measures club soda, garnish with a grapefruit twist,
and serve.

tahitian mule

makes **1**
glass **collins**

ice cubes
1 measure **amber rum**
2 teaspoons **lime juice**
1 tablespoon **orange liqueur**
3 measures **ginger beer**
lime and **orange slice**,
   to garnish

Fill a glass with ice. Pour rum, lime juice, orange liqueur, and ginger beer into the glass and stir.

Garnish with lime and orange slices and serve.

For Baijan Punch, fill a cocktail shaker with ice. Add 2 measures almond-infused rum (see page 12), 2 teaspoons ginger juice, 1 measure pineapple juice, 2 teaspoons falernum, 2 teaspoons lime juice, and 2 dashes Angostura bitters and shake. Strain into a collins glass filled with ice cubes and top up with 4 measures club soda. Garnish with a pineapple wedge or lime slice and serve.

mexican mule

makes **2**
glasses **highball**
equipment **muddler**

2 **limes**
2 dashes **sugar syrup**
crushed ice
2 measures **José Cuervo Gold tequila**
2 measures **Kahlúa coffee liqueur**
ginger ale, to top up

Cut the limes into wedges. Put half in each highball glass and muddle with the sugar syrup.

Fill each glass halfway with crushed ice, add the tequila and Kahlúa, stir, and top up with ginger ale.

For a Moscow Mule, put cracked ice from 6–8 ice cubes into a cocktail shaker, add 4 measures vodka and the juice of 4 limes, and shake well. Pour, without straining, into 2 highball glasses over ice and top up with ginger beer.

ginger fix

makes **1**
glass **collins**

ice cubes
1 measure **blended Scotch whisky**
1 measure **ginger wine**
2 dashes **Angostura bitters**
4 measures **club soda**
lemon wedge, to garnish

Fill the glass with ice cubes, add the remaining ingredients, and stir.

Garnish with a lemon wedge and serve.

For a Highland Punch, add 1 ½ measures blended Scotch whisky, 1 tablespoon Drambuie, 1 measure lemon juice, 1 tablespoon honey, 2 teaspoons fresh ginger juice, and 2 dashes Angostura bitters to a cocktail shaker. Shake, strain into a collins glass filled with ice cubes, and top up with 4 measures club soda. Garnish with crystallized ginger and serve.

sex on the beach

makes **2**

glasses **highball**

equipment **cocktail shaker, strainer**

ice cubes

2 measures **vodka**

2 measures **peach schnapps**

2 measures **cranberry juice**

2 measures **orange juice**

2 measures **pineapple juice** (optional)

To garnish

lemon wedges

lime wedges

Put 8–10 ice cubes into a cocktail shaker and add the vodka, schnapps, cranberry juice, orange juice, and pineapple juice (if used). Shake well.

Put 3–4 ice cubes into each highball glass and strain the cocktail over them. Garnish with lemon and lime wedges and serve.

For Sex in the Dunes, replace the cranberry juice and orange juice with 1 measure Chambord, shake well, and garnish each glass with pineapple chunks.

fizz & froth

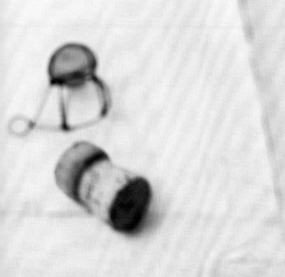

bellini

makes **1**
glass **flute**
equipment **food processor,
strainer**

½ **ripe white peach**
2 teaspoons **sugar syrup**
5 measures **prosecco**, chilled

Put the peach and sugar syrup into a food processor or blender and blend until smooth.

Strain into a flute glass, top with the prosecco, and serve.

For an Orchard Bellini, add 1 measure white peach puree, ½ teaspoon matcha green tea, 2 teaspoons sugar syrup, and 5 measures chilled prosecco to a flute glass, stir, and serve.

rossini

makes **1**

glass **flute**

equipment **food processor, strainer**

4 **strawberries**

2 teaspoons **sugar syrup**

5 measures **prosecco**, chilled

Put the strawberries and sugar syrup into a food processor or blender and blend until smooth.

Strain into a flute glass, top with the prosecco, and serve.

For a Parisian Fizz, add 4 teaspoons raspberry puree, 2 teaspoons passion fruit pulp, 1 teaspoon sugar syrup, 1 teaspoon pastis, and 4 measures chilled prosecco to a flute glass and stir. Garnish with a raspberry and serve.

bucks fizz

makes **1**
glass **flute**

2 measures **fresh orange
  juice**, chilled
1 measure **sloe gin**, chilled
2 measures **prosecco**, chilled
orange twist, to garnish

Pour all the ingredients into a flute glass, garnish with an orange twist. and serve.

For a St. Marks Fizz, add 1 measure Aperol, 1 measure pink grapefruit juice, 2 teaspoons passion fruit syrup, and 3 measures chilled prosecco to a wine glass full of ice cubes and stir. Garnish with a grapefruit wedge and serve.

french 75

makes **1**

glass **flute**

equipment **cocktail shaker,
    strainer**

1 measure **gin**

1 tablespoon **lemon juice**

1 tablespoon **sugar syrup**

4 measures **champagne**,
    chilled

lemon twist, to garnish

Add the gin, lemon juice, and sugar syrup to a cocktail shaker and shake.

Strain into a flute glass and top up with the champagne. Garnish with a lemon twist and serve.

For a French Afternoon, add 1 measure gin, 3 teaspoons camomile tea syrup (see page 9), 3 teaspoons lemon juice, and 2 dashes peach bitters to a cocktail shaker. Shake and strain into a flute glass. Top up with 4 measures chilled champagne, garnish with a lemon twist, and serve.

valencian sangria

makes **1**
glass **wine glass**

ice cubes
1 measure **brandy**
2 measures **blood orange
 juice**
1 pinch **pink peppercorns**
1 measure **sweet vermouth**
2 teaspoons **Campari**
2 measures **red wine**
2 measures **club soda**
orange slice, to garnish

Fill a wine glass with ice cubes. Add all the remaining ingredients and stir.

Garnish with an orange slice and serve.

For Bitter Sweet Sangria, fill a large wine glass with ice cubes, add 1 measure orange liqueur, 1 measure sweet vermouth, 2 teaspoons Campari, 2 measures red wine, 2 measures lemon-lime soda, and stir. Garnish with an orange slice and serve.

zan la cay

makes **1**

glass **flute**

equipment **cocktail shaker, muddler, strainer**

2 inch piece **cucumber**

1 **green cardamom pod**

1 tablespoon **crème de peche**

2 teaspoons **sugar syrup**

ice cubes

4 measures **champagne**, chilled

cucumber slice, to garnish

Muddle the cucumber and cardamom pod at the bottom of a cocktail shaker, then add the crème de peche and sugar syrup.

Add a couple of ice cubes, pour in the champagne, and stir before straining into a flute glass.

Garnish with a cucumber slice and serve.

For a Bali Fizz, add 1 measure bison grass vodka, 1 tablespoon peach juice, 1 green cardamom pod, 1 measure cucumber juice, 2 teaspoons lemon juice, and 2 teaspoons sugar syrup to a cocktail shaker. Shake, then strain into a flute glass. Top up with 3 measures chilled champagne, garnish with a cucumber slice, and serve.

ambika bellini

makes **1**
glass **flute**
equipment **food processor,
 strainer**

4 cubes **fresh mango**, about
 ¾ inch each
1 teaspoon **grenadine**
5 measures **prosecco**, chilled

Put the mango and grenadine into a food processor or blender and blend until smooth.

Strain into a flute glass, top with the prosecco, and serve.

For a Nehru, put 4 cubes fresh mango, 1 measure gin, and 5 pink peppercorns into a food processor or blender and blend until smooth. Strain into a flute glass, top up with 4 measures chilled prosecco, and serve.

cotter kir

makes **1**
glass **wine glass**

ice cubes
2 teaspoons **crème de cassis**
2 teaspoons **crème de framboise**
1 measure **cranberry juice**
3 measures **rosé wine**
3 measures **club soda**
raspberries, to garnish

Fill a wine glass with ice cubes. Add the remaining ingredients and stir.

Garnish with a couple of raspberries and serve.

For a Kir Royale, add 1 measure crème de cassis and 5 measures chilled prosecco to a flute glass and mix. Expel the oils from a lemon twist into the glass by twisting the zest over the cocktail, then drop the lemon twist into the glass and serve.

cobbler fizz

makes **1**
glass **flute**
equipment **cocktail shaker,
muddler, strainer**

3 slices **tangerine**
2 **raspberries**, plus extra
to garnish
2 teaspoons **sugar syrup**
1 measure **fino sherry**
4 measures **prosecco**, chilled

Add the tangerine, raspberries, and sugar syrup to a cocktail shaker and muddle.

Add the sherry and shake. Strain into a flute glass and top up with the prosecco.

Garnish with a raspberry and serve.

For a Royal Cobbler, add 1 tablespoon gin, 1 tablespoon fino sherry, 1 tablespoon raspberry & pineapple syrup (see page 10), and 2 teaspoons lemon juice to a cocktail shaker and shake. Strain into a flute glass. Top up with 3 measures chilled prosecco, garnish with an orange twist, and serve.

primrose fizz

makes **1**
glass **small wine glass**
equipment **muddler, strainer**

4 **mint leaves**
ice cubes
4 teaspoons **elderflower liqueur**
1 measure **apple juice**
4 measures **champagne**, chilled
apple slice, to garnish

Bruise the mint leaves and then place them in a wine glass.

Fill the glass with ice cubes, add the remaining ingredients, and stir. Garnish with an apple slice and serve.

For a Sunshine State, add 4 teaspoons gin, 3 teaspoons elderflower liqueur, 2 teaspoons lemon juice, 2 dashes peach bitters, 1 measure apple juice, and 3 mint leaves to a cocktail shaker and shake. Strain into a wine glass and top with 3 measures chilled prosecco. Garnish with a strawberry and serve.

long island iced tea

makes **2**

glasses **highball**

equipment **cocktail shaker,
    strainer**

1 measure **vodka**

1 measure **gin**

1 measure **white rum**

1 measure **tequila**

1 measure **Cointreau**

1 measure **lemon juice**

ice cubes

cola, to top up

lemon slices, to garnish

Put the vodka, gin, rum, tequila, Cointreau, and lemon juice into a cocktail shaker with some ice cubes and shake to mix.

Strain into 2 highball glasses filled with ice cubes and top up with cola. Garnish with lemon slices and serve.

For a Camber Sands Iced Tea, shake 4 measures lemon vodka with 1 cup of Earl Grey tea, 2 measures cranberry juice, 12 mint leaves, a dash of sugar syrup, some lemon juice, and plenty of ice. Strain over ice into 2 highball glasses and garnish with lemon slices and mint leaves.

golden apricot

makes **1**
glass **collins**
equipment **food processor,
 strainer**

3 tablespoons **rum**
1 tablespoon **apricot liqueur**
4 teaspoons **lime juice**
4 teaspoons **sugar syrup**
1 **egg yolk**
ice cubes
4 measures **club soda**
dried apricot, to garnish

Put the rum, apricot liqueur, lime juice, sugar syrup, and egg yolk into a food processor or blender and blend.

Strain into a glass and fill the glass with ice cubes before topping up with the club soda. Garnish with a dried apricot and serve.

For Wrong Island Spiced Tea, add 1 yellow tea bag to a cup of boiling water and let cool. Put 1 measure spiced rum, 2 teaspoons apricot liqueur, 1 teaspoon ginger juice, 1 tablespoon lime juice, 1 tablespoon sugar syrup, and 2 dashes Angostura bitters into a soda syphon. Add 4 measures of the cooled yellow tea and charge with carbon dioxide, following the manufacturer's instructions. Chill in the refrigerator before serving in an iced collins glass, garnished with crystallized ginger.

cuba libre

makes **2**

glasses **highball**

equipment **straws**

ice cubes

4 measures **golden rum**, such
as Havana Club 3-year-old

juice of **1 lime**

cola, to top up

lime wedges

Fill 2 highball glasses with ice cubes. Pour the rum over
and lime juice the ice and stir.

Top up with cola, garnish with lime wedges, and serve
with straws.

For a Lucha Libre, fill a tall collins glass with ice cubes.
Add 2 measures each blanco tequila, cola, club soda,
½ measure each triple sec and lime juice, and
2 dashes orange bitters. Stir to mix and garnish
with 2 lime wedges.

ginny gin fizz

makes **1**
glass **wine glass**
equipment **cocktail shaker,**
  strainer

1 **camomile tea bag**
2 measures **gin**
1 measure **sugar syrup**
1 measure **lemon juice**
1 tablespoon **egg white**
ice cubes
3 measures **club soda**
lemon twist, to garnish

Put the tea bag and gin into a cocktail shaker and let infuse for 2 minutes. Remove the tea bag, add the sugar syrup, lemon juice, and egg white. Fill the shaker with ice cubes.

Shake and strain into a wine glass filled with ice cubes and top up with the club soda.

Garnish with a lemon twist and serve.

For a Strawberry Fields, put 1 camomile tea bag and 2 measures gin in a cocktail shaker and let infuse for 2 minutes. Remove the tea bag, add 1 measure strawberry puree, 2 teaspoons lemon juice, 1 measure heavy cream, and 1 tablespoon egg white to the shaker. Shake and strain into a wine glass and top up with 4 measures chilled club soda. Garnish with a strawberry and serve.

riviera fizz

makes **2**

glasses **flutes**

equipment **cocktail shaker, strainer**

3 measures **sloe gin**

1 measure **lemon juice**

1 measure **sugar syrup**

ice cubes

chilled **champagne**, to top up

lemon twists, to garnish

Put the sloe gin, lemon juice, and sugar syrup into a cocktail shaker and add some ice cubes.

Shake and strain into 2 chilled flutes. Top up with champagne, stir, garnish each glass with a lemon twist, and serve.

For a Classic Champagne Cocktail, put a sugar cube into each flute, saturate it with Angostura bitters, then add 1 measure of brandy. Top up with chilled champagne and serve.

mandarin 75

makes **1**
glass **flute**

1 tablespoon **mandarin oleo-saccharum** (see page 10)
1 measure **orange juice**, chilled
4 measures **champagne**, chilled
orange twist, to garnish

Add the oleo-saccharum to a flute and top with chilled champagne.

Stir gently and garnish with an orange twist.

For a Tanka Cobbler, add 1 tablespoon mandarin oleo-saccharum (see page 10), 3 raspberries, 1 measure fino sherry, 1 measure chilled blood orange juice, and 3 measures chilled champagne to a cocktail shaker and shake. Strain into a flute glass, garnish with a raspberry, and serve.

low-calorie cocktails

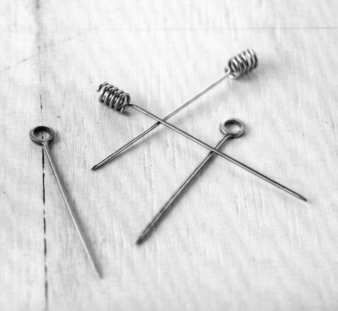

rum collins

makes **1**
glass **collins**

2 measures **white rum**
1 teaspoon **superfine sugar**
1 dash **orange bitters**
2 teaspoons **lemon juice**
ice cubes
3 measures **club soda**
lemon and **orange wedges**,
   to garnish

Add the rum and sugar to a glass and stir until the sugar has dissolved. Add the orange bitters and lemon juice.

Fill the glass with ice cubes, top up with the club soda, then stir. Garnish with a lemon and orange wedge and serve.

For a Baijan Swizzle, add 1 measure white rum, 1 tablespoon falernum, 4 teaspoons lime juice, 5 mint leaves, and 2 dashes Angostura bitters to a collins glass filled halfway with crushed ice and swizzle the drink by spinning a bar spoon between the two flat palms of your hand. Top the glass with crushed ice, garnish with a mint sprig and serve.

bitter spring

makes **1**
glass **old-fashioned glass**

1 measure **Aperol**
2 measures **grapefruit juice**
4 measures **club soda**
ice cubes
grapefruit wedge, to garnish

Add the Aperol, grapefruit juice, and club soda to wine glass full of ice cubes.

Stir, garnish with a grapefruit wedge, and serve.

For a Venetian Sling, add 1 measure Aperol, 3 teaspoons orange & fennel seed shrub (see page 11), 2 teaspoons lemon juice, 1 measure fresh orange juice, 3 measures white wine, and 2 measures club soda to a wine glass full of ice cubes and stir. Garnish with an orange slice and serve.

cucumber rangoon

makes **1**
glass **wine glass**

ice cubes
2 measures **Pimm's No. 1**
2 measures **cucumber juice**
2 teaspoons **ginger juice**
3 measures **club soda**
cucumber slice, to garnish

Fill a glass with ice cubes, add the remaining ingredients, and stir.

Garnish with a cucumber slice and serve.

For a Rum Rangoon, add 1 measure cucumber-infused white rum (see page 12), 1 measure umeshu, 2 dashes Angostura bitters, 2 measures apple juice, and 4 measures club soda to a collins glass full of ice and stir. Garnish with a cucumber slice and serve.

watermelon smash

makes **1**

glass **old-fashioned**

equipment **food processor**

1 measure **tequila**

4 chunks **watermelon**

5 **mint leaves**, plus an extra
 sprig, to garnish

1 teaspoon **agave syrup**

1 cup crushed **ice**

Add all the ingredients to a food processor or blender and blend until smooth.

Pour into a glass, garnish with a mint sprig, and serve.

For a Watermelon Sangrita, add 1 measure tequila, 5 chunks watermelon, 3 dashes Tabasco, 1 sprig cilantro, and 2 skinned green tomatoes to a food processor or blender and blend until smooth. Pour into an old-fashioned glass full of ice cubes. Garnish with a watermelon wedge and serve.

fino highball

makes **1**

glass **collins**

equipment **cocktail shaker, muddler, strainer**

4 slices **clementine**
2 slices **lemon**
1 measure **gin**
1 measure **fino sherry**
2 teaspoons **passion fruit syrup**
ice cubes
2 measures **low-calorie tonic water**
crushed ice
lemon wedge, to garnish

Muddle the fruit in a cocktail shaker and add the gin, sherry, and passion fruit syrup. Fill the cocktail shaker with ice cubes. Shake, then strain into a glass. Add the tonic water and fill the glass with crushed ice. Garnish with a lemon wedge and serve.

For a Citrus Highball, put 1 measure gin and 1 citrus tea bag into a collins glass and let infuse for 2 minutes. Remove the tea bag, fill the glass with ice cubes, and top up with 4 measures low-calorie tonic water. Stir, then garnish with a lime or orange wedge and serve.

mango ricky

makes **1**

glass **collins**

5 **basil leaves**, plus extra
   leaves, to garnish
2 **lime wedges**
1 measure **mango-infused
   gin** (see page 13)
2 teaspoons **sugar syrup**
2 measures **club soda**
crushed ice

Coarsely tear the basil leaves and add to a glass.

Squeeze the lime wedges over the glass and then
add them to the glass. Add the gin, sugar syrup, and
club soda, then top up the glass with crushed ice.

Garnish with basil leaves and serve.

For a Peppermint Ricky, put 1 measure vodka and
1 peppermint tea bag into a collins glass and let infuse
for 3 minutes. Remove the tea bag and add ice cubes
to fill the glass. Add 3 lime wedges and 4 measures
club soda and stir. Garnish with an extra wedge of
lime and serve.

spiced berry julep

makes **1**

glass **collins**

equipment **muddler**

1 tablespoon **frozen mixed berries**, plus extra to garnish

1 measure **cinnamon & nutmeg-infused bourbon** (see page 12)

6 **mint leaves**, plus an extra sprig, to garnish

2 teaspoons **sugar syrup**

crushed ice

Put the berries, bourbon, and mint into a glass and muddle.

Let stand for 5 minutes, then add the sugar syrup, fill the glass halfway with crushed ice, and churn with the muddler.

When it is thoroughly mixed, top the glass with crushed ice. Garnish with frozen berries and serve.

For a Mint Julep, put 1 measure bourbon and 6 mint leaves into a collins glass and let infuse for 10 minutes. Add 2 teaspoons sugar syrup and fill the glass halfway with crushed ice before churning with a muddler. When it is thoroughly mixed, fill the glass with crushed ice. Garnish with a mint sprig and serve.

long blush

makes **1**
glass **collins**
equipment **cocktail shaker,
  strainer**

1 measure **vodka**
2 teaspoons **honey**
1 measure **pomegranate juice**
2 teaspoons **lime juice**
1 measure **rose wine**
5 **mint leaves**
2 measures **club soda**
crushed ice
mint sprig and **pomegranate
  seeds**, to garnish

Add the vodka, honey, pomegranate and lime juices, wine, and mint leaves to a cocktail shaker and shake.

Strain into glass and add the club soda. Top up the glass with crushed ice, garnish with a mint sprig and some pomegranate seeds, and serve.

For a Passion Fruit Spritz, add 4 measures white wine, 2 teaspoons honey syrup, the pulp of 1 passion fruit, and 3 measures club soda to a wine glass full of ice cubes and stir. Garnish with a passion fruit wedge and serve.

spagliagto

makes **1**
glass **old-fashioned**

ice cubes
1 measure **Campari**
1 measure **sweet vermouth**
2 measures **prosecco**, chilled
orange slice, to garnish

Fill a glass with ice cubes. Add the Campari, sweet vermouth, and prosecco and stir.

Garnish with an orange slice and serve.

For an Italian New Wave, infuse 1 teaspoon of black peppercorns in 1 measure sweet vermouth for 30 minutes, then remove the peppercorns. Add the infused sweet vermouth, 1 measure pineapple-infused Campari (see page 13), and 2 measures prosecco to an old-fashioned glass full of ice cubes and stir. Garnish with a pineapple wedge and serve.

pisco collins

makes **1**
glass **collins**

ice cubes
1 measure **pisco**
2 teaspoons **sugar syrup**
2 teaspoons **lemon juice**
4 measures **club soda**
2 dashes **peach bitters**
lemon wedge, to garnish

Fill a glass with ice cubes. Add the remaining ingredients and stir.

Garnish with a lemon wedge and serve.

For a Mocking Bird, put 2 kumquats, cut into quarters, 2 teaspoons elderflower syrup, and 2 teaspoons sugar syrup into a cocktail shaker and muddle. Add 1 measure grappa and 4 teaspoons lemon juice, fill the shaker with ice cubes, and shake. Strain into a collins glass filled with ice cubes and top up with 4 measures club soda. Garnish with a whole kumquat and serve.

mojito

makes **2**
glasses **highball**
equipment **muddler**

16 **mint leaves**, plus sprigs
   to garnish
1 **lime**, cut into wedges
4 teaspoons **sugar**
crushed ice
5 measures **white rum**
club soda, to top up

Muddle the mint leaves, lime, and sugar in the bottom of 2 highball glasses and fill with crushed ice.

Add the rum, stir, and top up with club soda. Garnish with mint sprigs and serve.

For a Limon Mojito, muddle the quarters of 2 limes with 4 teaspoons packed light brown sugar and 16 mint leaves in the bottom of 2 highball glasses, then add 4 measures Limon Bacardi. Stir and top up with club soda, if desired. Garnish with lemon and lime slices and drink through straws.

dirty sanchez

makes **2**

glasses **martini**

equipment **mixing glass, strainer**

ice cubes

4 teaspoons **Noilly Prat**

4 measures **gold tequila**

4 teaspoons **liquid from a jar of black ripe olives**

4 **black ripe olives**, to garnish

Fill a mixing glass with ice cubes and add the Noilly Prat. Stir to coat the ice thoroughly, then pour away the excess vermouth.

Add the tequila and olive liquid and stir until thoroughly chilled. Strain into 2 chilled martini glasses, garnish with olives, and serve.

For a Pancho Villa, shake 2 measures tequila with 1 measure Tia Maria, 2 teaspoons Cointreau, and plenty of ice, then strain into chilled martini glasses.

pink sangria

makes **1**
glass **wine glass**

3 measures **rose wine**
2 teaspoons **agave syrup**
ice cubes
2 measures **pomegranate juice**
2 measures **lemon verbena tea**
2 measures **club soda**
pink grapefruit slice, to garnish

Pour the rose wine into a glass, add 1 teaspoon of the agave syrup, and stir until it dissolves.

Fill the glass with ice cubes and add the remaining agave syrup, the pomegranate juice, lemon verbena tea, and club soda.

Garnish with a slice of pink grapefruit and serve.

For Poppin's Gin Fizz, to serve 4, add 1 ½ measures agave syrup and 4 measures gin to a pitcher and stir until the agave syrup dissolves. Fill the pitcher with ice cubes, add 1 cup hibiscus tea, 4 measures pink grapefruit juice, and 1 cup sparkling wine, and stir. Garnish with raspberries and serve.

martinis &
shorts

whisky sour

makes **1**

glass **old-fashioned**

equipment **cocktail shaker, strainer**

ice cubes

2 measures **Scotch whisky**

1 measure **lemon juice**

1 measure **sugar syrup**

lemon wedge and **lemon zest spirals**, to garnish

Fill a cocktail shaker with ice cubes. Add the remaining ingredients and shake.

Strain into a glass filled with ice cubes, garnish with a lemon wedge and a lemon zest spiral, and serve.

For a Penicillin, add 2 measures any Scotch whisky, 2 teaspoons Islay whisky, 2 teaspoons ginger juice, 1 measure sugar syrup, and 1 measure lemon juice to a cocktail shaker full of ice cubes. Shake and strain into an old-fashioned glass filled with ice cubes. Garnish with a lemon wedge and serve.

southside

makes **1**

glass **martini**

equipment **cocktail shaker, strainer**

ice cubes

2 measures **gin**

4 teaspoons **lime juice**

4 teaspoons **sugar syrup**

5 **mint leaves**, plus extra, to garnish

Add all the ingredients to a cocktail shaker.

Shake and strain into a glass. Garnish with a mint leaf and serve.

For a Southside Royale, add 2 measures gin, 4 slices cucumber, 4 mint leaves, 1 tablespoon lime juice, 1 tablespoon sugar syrup, and ice cubes to a cocktail shaker. Shake and strain into a martini glass. Top up with 1 measure chilled prosecco, garnish with mint leaf, and serve.

jack rose

makes **1**

glass **martini**

equipment **cocktail shaker, strainer**

ice cubes

2 measures **apple brandy**

1 tablespoon **grenadine**

4 teaspoons **lemon juice**

Add all the ingredients to a cocktail shaker.

Shake, strain into a glass, and serve.

For a Stone Jack Sour, add 2 measures apple brandy, 1 measure Triple Sec, 1 measure blood orange juice, 2 dashes orange bitters, and 2 teaspoons lemon juice to a cocktail shaker filled with ice cubes. Shake and strain into an old-fashioned glass filled with ice cubes. Garnish with an orange wedge and serve.

daiquiri

makes **1**
glass **martini**
equipment **cocktail shaker,
  strainer**

ice cubes
2 measures **light rum**
1 measure **sugar syrup**
1 measure **lime juice**
lime wedge, to garnish

Add all the ingredients to a cocktail shaker.

Shake and strain into a glass. Garnish with a lime wedge and serve.

For a Baijan Daiquiri, add ice cubes, 2 measures amber rum, 2 teaspoons Campari, 4 teaspoons lime juice, 1 tablespoon sugar syrup, and 1 measure pineapple juice to a cocktail shaker. Shake and strain into a martini glass. Garnish with a lime wedge and serve.

strawberry daiquiri

makes **1**

glass **martini**

equipment **muddler, cocktail shaker, strainer**

3 **strawberries**, hulled

dash of **strawberry syrup**

6 **mint leaves**, plus a sprig to garnish

2 measures **golden rum**

2 measures **lime juice**

ice cubes

strawberry slice, to garnish

Muddle the strawberries, syrup, and mint leaves in the bottom of a cocktail shaker.

Add the rum and lime juice, shake with ice, and double-strain into a chilled martini glass. Garnish with a strawberry slice and a sprig of mint.

For a Melon Daiquiri, shake 2 measures rum, 1 measure lime juice, and ½ measure Midori with plenty of crushed ice, then strain into a chilled martini glass. Garnish with a small wedge of melon.

old-fashioned

makes **1**
glass **old-fashioned**

ice cubes
2 measures **bourbon**
1 teaspoon **sugar syrup**
1 dash **orange bitters**
1 dash **Angostura bitters**
orange twist, to garnish

Fill a glass halfway with ice cubes. Add the remaining ingredients to the glass and stir for 1 minute.

Fill the glass with more ice cubes. Garnish with an orange twist and serve.

For an Old-Fashioned at Dusk, add 2 measures tequila, 2 teaspoons Islay whisky, 1 teaspoon agave syrup, and 2 dashes Angostura bitters to an old-fashioned glass full of ice cubes and stir. Garnish with an orange twist and serve.

rum old-fashioned

makes **2**
glasses **old-fashioned**

6 **ice cubes**
2 dashes **Angostura bitters**
2 dashes **lime bitters**
2 teaspoons **superfine sugar**
1 measure **water**
4 measures **white rum**
1 measure **dark rum**
lime zest twists, to garnish

Stir 1 ice cube with a dash of both bitters, 1 teaspoon sugar, and half the water in each old-fashioned glass until the sugar has dissolved.

Add the white rum, stir, and add the remaining ice cubes. Add the dark rum and stir again. Garnish each glass with a lime zest twist and serve.

For a Rum Refashioned, put a brown sugar cube in each old-fashioned glass, splash it with some Angostura bitters, then add 2 ice cubes and 2 measures aged rum to each glass, stir well, and add sugar syrup to taste.

french pink lady

makes **1**
glass **martini**
equipment **cocktail shaker,
   muddler, strainer**

2 measures **gin**
4 **raspberries**
1 measure **Triple Sec**
1 tablespoon **lime juice**
1 teaspoon **pastis**
ice cubes
lime wedge, to garnish

Add the gin, raspberries, Triple Sec, lime juice, and
pastis to a cocktail shaker and muddle.

Fill the shaker with ice and shake, then strain into
a glass. Garnish with a lime wedge and serve.

For a Margarita, add 2 measures tequila, 1 measure
Triple Sec, and 1 tablespoon lime juice to a cocktail
shaker. Fill the shaker with ice cubes and shake.
Strain into a martini glass. Garnish with a lime
wedge and serve.

classic martini

makes **2**

glasses **martini**

equipment **mixing glass, strainer**

ice cubes

1 measure **dry vermouth**

6 measures **gin**

stuffed green olives, to garnish

Put 10–12 ice cubes into a mixing glass.

Pour the vermouth and gin over the ice cubes and stir (never shake) vigorously and evenly without splashing. Strain into 2 chilled martini glasses, garnish each with a green olive, and serve.

For a Smoky Martini, put some ice cubes into a mixing glass, add ½ measure dry vermouth, and stir until the ice cubes are well coated. Pour in 4 measures gin and 2 measures sloe gin, then add 10 drops orange bitters. Stir well, then strain into 2 chilled cocktail glasses and add an orange twist to each.

negroni

makes **1**
glass **old-fashioned**

ice cubes
1 measure **gin**
1 measure **sweet vermouth**
1 measure **Campari**
orange wedge, to garnish

Fill a glass with ice cubes and add the remaining ingredients to a glass and stir.

Garnish with an orange wedge and serve.

For a Primera, fill an old-fashioned glass with ice cubes. Add 1 ½ measures tequila, 4 teaspoons Aperol, 2 teaspoons sweet vermouth, 1 tablespoon dry vermouth, and 2 dashes orange bitters. Stir and serve.

martinez

makes **1**
glass **martini**

ice cubes
2 measures **gin**
1 tablespoon **sweet vermouth**
2 teaspoons **orange liqueur**
2 dashes **Angostura bitters**
orange twist, to garnish

Fill a glass with ice and add the remaining ingredients.

Stir, garnish with an orange twist, and serve.

For a Dutch Rose, add 1 ½ measures vodka, 2 teaspoons orange liqueur, 2 teaspoons dry vermouth, 2 dashes orange bitters, 1 dash orange blossom water, and 1 teaspoon grenadine to a martini glass filled with ice cubes and stir. Garnish with an orange twist and serve.

lychee martini

makes **1**
glass **martini**
equipment **cocktail shaker,
  muddler, strainer**

ice cubes
2 measures **vodka**
3 **lychees**, plus extra,
   to garnish
1 measure **Triple Sec**
1 tablespoon **lemon juice**

Add all the ingredients to a cocktail shaker and muddle.

Shake, then strain into a glass. Garnish with a lychee and serve.

For an Annabella, add ice cubes, 2 measures vodka, ½ plum, 2 lychees, 4 teaspoons rose syrup (see page 9), and 4 teaspoons lemon juice to a cocktail shaker and muddle. Shake, then strain into a martini glass. Garnish with a lychee and serve.

jaffa

makes **2**
glasses **martini**
equipment **cocktail shaker,
strainer**

ice cubes
2 measures **brandy**
2 measures **dark crème de
cacao**
2 measures **light cream**
1 measure **Mandarine
Napoléon**
4 dashes **orange bitters**
**orange-flavored chocolate
shavings,** to garnish

Fill a cocktail shaker halfway with ice cubes. Add the remaining ingredients and shake until a frost forms on the outside of the shaker.

Strain into 2 chilled martini glasses, garnish with orange-flavored chocolate shavings, and serve.

For a Brandy Alexander, shake together 2 measures each of brandy, dark crème de cacao, and light cream. Strain into chilled martini glasses and garnish with some crumbled chocolate shavings.

cosmopolitan

makes **1**
glass **martini**
equipment **cocktail shaker,
 strainer**

ice cubes
1 ½ measures **lemon vodka**
4 teaspoons **Triple Sec**
1 tablespoon **lime juice**
1 measure **cranberry juice**
lime wedge, to garnish

Add all the ingredients to a cocktail shaker.

Shake and strain into a glass. Garnish with a lime wedge and serve.

For a Williamsburg, add ice cubes, 1 ½ measures star anise-infused vodka (see page 13), 2 teaspoons crème de framboise, 2 teaspoons Triple Sec, 1 tablespoon lime juice, and 1 measure cranberry juice to a cocktail shaker and shake. Strain into a martini glass, garnish with a raspberry, and serve.

pisco punch

makes **1**

glass **wine glass**

equipment **cocktail shaker, muddler, strainer**

2 measures **pisco**

2 **pineapple chunks**

1 measure **orange juice**

4 teaspoons **lime juice**

2 teaspoons **falernum**

2 teaspoons **sugar syrup**

2 dashes **Angostura bitters**

ice cubes

pineapple wedge and **leaf**, to garnish

Add all the ingredients to a cocktail shaker and muddle.

Shake, then strain into a glass filled with ice cubes. Garnish with a pineapple wedge and serve.

For a Pisco Sour, add 2 measures pisco, 1 measure lime juice, 1 measure sugar syrup, 1 tablespoon egg white, and 3 dashes Angostura Bitters to a cocktail shaker. Shake, then strain into a wine glass filled with ice cubes and serve.

abc cocktail

makes **1**
glass **martini**
equipment **cocktail shaker,
  strainer**

ice cubes
1 measure **VSOP Cognac**
1 measure **tawny port**
2 teaspoons **maraschino
  liqueur**
6 **mint leaves**, plus extra,
  to garnish

Add all the ingredients to a cocktail shaker.

Shake and strain into a glass. Garnish with a mint leaf and serve.

For a Port Stinger, add ice cubes, 2 measures tawny port, 2 teaspoons crème de framboise, 2 teaspoons crème de cassis, 3 raspberries, and 4 mint leaves to a cocktail shaker. Shake and strain into a martini glass. Garnish with a mint leaf and serve.

godmother

makes **2**
glasses **old-fashioned**

4–6 **ice cubes**, cracked
3 measures **vodka**
1 measure **Amaretto
di Saronno**

Put the cracked ice into 2 old-fashioned glasses.

Add the vodka and Amaretto, stir lightly to mix, and serve.

For a St. Petersburg, replace the Amaretto with the same amount of Chartreuse.

sombrero

makes **2**

glasses **martini**

equipment **cocktail shaker,
    strainer**

hot cocoa mix

1½ measures **tequila**

1½ measures **white crème
    de cacao**

¾ cup **light cream**

ice cubes

Dampen the rim of 2 chilled martini glasses and dip them into the hot cocoa mix.

Pour the tequila, crème de cacao, cream, and grenadine into a cocktail shaker and add 8–10 ice cubes. Shake vigorously for 10 seconds, then strain into the chilled martini glasses.

For a Silk Stocking, make a Sombrero, adding 4 teaspoons grenadine to the cocktail shaker. Garnish with some grated nutmeg before serving.

rising sun

makes **2**
glasses **old-fashioned**
equipment **cocktail shaker,
   strainer**

ice cubes
4 measures **vodka**
4 teaspoons **passion fruit
   syrup**
6 measures **grapefruit juice**
pink grapefruit slices,
   to garnish

Fill a cocktail shaker halfway with ice cubes and put
6–8 ice cubes into each old-fashioned glass.

Add all the remaining ingredients to the shaker and
shake until a frost forms on the outside of the shaker.
Strain over the ice in the glasses, garnish each with
a pink grapefruit slice, and serve.

For a Harvey Wallbanger, float 1 teaspoon Galliano
over a mixture of 1 measure vodka and 3 measures
orange juice and plenty of ice.

grasshopper

makes **2**

glasses **martini**
equipment **bar spoon**

2 measures **crème de cacao**
2 measures **crème de menthe**
mint sprigs, to garnish

Pour the crème de cacao into 2 martini glasses.

Using the back of a bar spoon, float the crème de menthe over the crème de cacao to create a separate layer. Garnish with mint sprigs and serve.

For a Banshee, shake together 2 measures crème de cacao with 2 measures crème de banane, 2 measures light cream, and plenty of crushed ice, then strain into 2 chilled martini glasses.

valentine martini

makes **2**
glasses **martini**
equipment **cocktail shaker,
   strainer**

ice cubes
4 measures **raspberry vodka**
12 **raspberries**, plus extra
   to garnish
1 measure **lime juice**
2 dashes **sugar syrup**
lime zest spirals, to garnish

Fill a cocktail shaker halfway with ice cubes. Add all the remaining ingredients and shake until a frost forms on the outside of the shaker. Double-strain into 2 chilled martini glasses.

Garnish with raspberries and lime zest spirals on toothpicks and serve.

For Watermelon Martinis, add the juice of ½ lime, 8 chunks watermelon, 3 measures vodka, 1 measure passion fruit liqueur, and 1 dash cranberry juice to a cocktail shaker. Add ice cubes and shake. Strain into 2 chilled martini glasses and garnish each glass with a watermelon wedge.

gin garden martini

makes **2**

glasses **martini**

equipment **muddler, cocktail shaker, strainer**

½ **cucumber**, peeled and chopped, plus extra slices to garnish

1 measure **elderflower syrup**

4 measures **gin**

2 measures **apple cider**

ice cubes

Muddle the cucumber in the bottom of a cocktail shaker with the elderflower syrup.

Add the gin, apple cider, and some ice cubes. Shake and double-strain into 2 chilled martini glasses, garnish with peeled cucumber slices, and serve.

For Apple Martinis, mix 4 measures vodka, 2 measures apple schnapps, and 2 tablespoons applesauce in a cocktail shaker with plenty of ice cubes. Add a generous dash of lime juice and a pinch of ground cinnamon, shake, and strain into 2 chilled martini glasses garnished with red apple wedges.

moon river

makes **2**
glasses **martini**
equipment **cocktail shaker,
  strainer**

ice cubes
1 measure **dry gin**
1 measure **apricot brandy**
1 measure **Cointreau**
½ measure **Galliano**
½ measure **lemon juice**
maraschino cherries,
  to garnish

Put some ice cubes into a cocktail shaker. Pour the gin, apricot brandy, Cointreau, Galliano, and lemon juice over the ice.

Shake, then strain into 2 large chilled martini glasses. Garnish each with a cherry.

For Maiden's Prayers, pour 4 measures gin into a cocktail shaker with some ice, then add 4 measures Cointreau and 2 measures orange juice. Shake well, then strain into 2 chilled martini glasses.

blanc mont blanc

makes **1**

glass **martini**

equipment **cocktail shaker, muddler, strainer**

5 **white grapes**, plus extra to garnish

1 measure **vodka**

1 measure **blanc vermouth**

1 measure **lemon juice**

1 measure **sugar syrup**

ice cubes

Muddle the grapes at the bottom of a cocktail shaker. Add the vodka, blanc vermouth, lemon juice, and sugar syrup.

Fill the shaker with ice cubes. Shake and strain into a martini glass. Garnish with grapes and serve.

For a Copa Kaye, muddle 5 red grapes at the bottom of cocktail shaker. Add 2 measures caçhaca, 1 measure lime juice, 1 measure sugar syrup, and the pulp of ½ passion fruit. Fill the shaker with ice cubes and shake. Strain into a chilled martini glass, garnish with red grapes, and serve.

pressed &
squeezed

fresh paloma

makes **1**

glass **collins**

equipment **juicer**

½ **pink grapefruit**, peeled

ice cubes

2 measures **blanco tequila**

2 measures **club soda**

1 teaspoon **agave syrup**

pink grapefruit wedge,
   to garnish

Juice the pink grapefruit and add the juice to a glass full of ice cubes.

Add the remaining ingredients to the glass, garnish with a grapefruit wedge, and serve.

For a Paloma Verde, juice a 2 inch piece cucumber, ½ pink grapefruit, 5 pineapple chunks, and 1 sprig cilantro. Pour the juice into a collins glass full of ice cubes, then add 2 measures tequila and 2 measures club soda. Garnish with a grapefruit wedge and serve.

stone fence

makes **1**
glass **old-fashioned**
equipment **juicer**

1 **crisp apple**, plus an **apple
  slice**, to garnish
ice cubes
2 measures **rye whiskey**
1 measure **club soda**

Juice the apple and pour into a glass full of ice cubes.

Add the whiskey and club soda. Garnish with an apple slice and serve.

For a Stone Stairs, juice ½ Granny Smith apple and ½ pear. Pour the juice into an old-fashioned glass full of ice cubes, add 1 ½ measures Scotch whisky, 2 teaspoons Bénédictine, and 1 measure club soda. Garnish with a pear slice and serve.

pink cooler

makes **1**
glass **old-fashioned**
equipment **cocktail shaker,
  muddler, strainer**

5 chunks **watermelon,**
  plus extra, to garnish
2 measures **lemon vodka**
ice cubes
2 measures **bitter lemon**

Add the watermelon to a cocktail shaker and muddle. Add the vodka and shake.

Strain into a glass full of ice cubes and top up with the bitter lemon. Garnish with a chunk of watermelon and serve.

For a Watermelon Spritz, add 4 chunks watermelon to a cocktail shaker and muddle. Add the lemon vodka with 1 measure apple juice, 1 sprig mint, 4 teaspoons lemon juice, and 1 tablespoon agave syrup. Shake and strain into a collins glass full of ice cubes and top up with 2 measures club soda. Garnish with a watermelon slice and serve.

william's pear

makes **1**
glass **old-fashioned**
equipment **cocktail shaker,
   muddler, strainer**

½ **ripe pear** cut into chunks,
   plus an extra slice, to garnish
1 tablespoon **red currant
   or seedless raspberry
   preserves**
2 measures **bourbon**
4 teaspoons **lemon juice**
2 teaspoons **sugar syrup**
ice cubes

Add the pear and preserves to a cocktail shaker and muddle.

Add the remaining ingredients and shake. Strain into a glass full of ice cubes, garnish with pear slices, and serve.

For Spiced Pear Punch, add ½ ripe pear, cut in to chunks, and 10 red currants or raspberries to a cocktail shaker and muddle. Add 1½ measures bourbon, 2 teaspoons Bénédictine, 2 teaspoons nutmeg syrup, and 2 teaspoons lemon juice and shake. Strain into an old-fashioned glass full of ice cubes, garnish with pear slices, and serve.

kiwi smash

makes **1**
glass **old-fashioned**
equipment **muddler**

½ **kiwifruit**, quartered, plus
   an extra slice, to garnish
4 slices **lemon**
4 teaspoons **sugar syrup**
2 measures **gin**
1 sprig **cilantro**
crushed ice

Add the kiwifruit, lemon, and sugar syrup to a glass and muddle. Add the gin and cilantro and fill the glass halfway with crushed ice.

Churn with the muddler until thoroughly mixed. Top up with more crushed ice, garnish with a kiwifruit slice, and serve.

For a Green Bay Colada, add 2 measures gin, ½ kiwifruit, peeled, 4 (2 inch) cantaloupe cubes, 1 sprig cilantro, 1 teaspoon ginger juice, 2 teaspoons lemon juice, 1 measure agave syrup, and 1 cup ice cubes to a food processor or blender and blend until smooth. Pour into a collins glass, garnish with a kiwi slice, and serve.

sherry punch

makes **1**
glass **old-fashioned**
equipment **cocktail shaker,
    muddler, strainer**

5 **pineapple** chunks
5 **raspberries**, plus extra
    to garnish
3 **lemon slices**
2 measures **fino sherry**
2 teaspoons **sugar syrup**
crushed ice

To garnish
pineapple wedge
raspberry

Add the pineapple chunks, raspberries, lemon slices, and sugar syrup to a cocktail shaker and muddle.

Add the sherry and shake. Strain into a glass full of crushed ice, garnish with a pineapple wedge and a raspberry, and serve.

For a Cobbled Summer, add 6 (½ inch) pineapple cubes to a cocktail shaker and muddle. Add 2 tablespoons fino sherry, 4 teaspoons gin, 1 tablespoon raspberry syrup, 1 tablespoon lemon juice, and 2 teaspoons sugar syrup and shake. Strain into a collins glass filled with ice cubes, garnish with a raspberry, and serve.

cloudy cooler

makes **1**

glass **collins**

equipment **cocktail shaker,
muddler, strainer**

5 **white grapes**, plus extra
to garnish

4 measures **white wine**

2 measures **apple cider**

1 teaspoon **passion
fruit syrup**

2 measures **club soda**

ice cubes

Add the grapes to a cocktail shaker and muddle.

Add the wine, apple cider, and passion fruit syrup to
the shaker and shake.

Strain into a glass full of ice cubes and top with the
club soda. Garnish with a few grapes and serve.

For a Camomile Sangria, add 1 camomile tea bag
and 1 measure vodka to a cocktail shaker and let
infuse for 3 minutes. Remove the tea bag, add 5 white
grapes, and muddle, Then add 2 measures white wine,
2 teaspoons passion fruit syrup, and 1 teaspoon lemon
juice. Shake and strain into a collins glass full of ice
cubes, top up with 2 measures club soda, garnish with
an apple wedge, and serve.

betsy

makes **2**

glass **old-fashioned**

equipment **food processor**

2 measures **gin** or **vodka**

4 teaspoons **lime juice**

1 measure **sugar syrup**

2 **strawberries**, plus extra,
    to garnish

1 sprig **cilantro**

1 cup **ice cubes**

Add all the ingredients to a food processor or blender and blend until smooth.

Pour into 2 glasses, garnish each with a strawberry, and serve.

For a West Side Pink Flamingo, add ½ cup gin or vodka, 1 measure lime juice, 1 measure strawberry syrup (see page 9), 2 measures strawberry puree, 1 cup rose wine, 2 sprigs mint, and 1 cup watermelon juice to a food processor or blender and give it short pulses to coarsely chop the mint. Pour into a shallow freezer container and freeze for 24 hours. Remove from the freezer and stir with a fork to create a granita. Spoon into 2 wine glasses, garnish with a mint sprig each, and serve with spoon.

nonalcoholic jade's cooler

makes **1**
glass **old-fashioned**
equipment **juicer**

1 **apple**
2 inch piece **cucumber**
1 **mint sprig**
ice cubes
1 tablespoon **elderflower syrup**
2 measures **club soda**
apple slice or **mint sprig**, to garnish

Juice the apple, cucumber, and mint. Pour the juice into a glass full of ice cubes, add the elderflower syrup, stir, and top up with the club soda. Garnish with an apple slice or mint sprig and serve.

For an Orchard Fizz, another alcohol-free cocktail, juice 1 apple, a 2 inch piece cucumber, a ½ inch piece fresh ginger root, peeled, 2 sprigs mint, and 1 stick celery. Pour the juice into a soda syphon and add 2 measures elderflower syrup and 2 measures water. Add carbon dioxide, following the manufacturer's directions. Chill the charged vessel in the refrigerator for 1 hour, then pour the cocktail into a flute glass, garnish with a mint sprig, and serve.

nonalcoholic strawberry smash

makes **1**

glass **collins**

equipment **juicer**

6 **strawberries**

1 **apple**

2 **sticks celery**

1 **sprig mint**

ice cubes

apple slices, to garnish

Juice all the ingredients and pour the juice into a glass full of ice cubes.

Garnish with a fan of apple slices and serve.

For a Strawberry Fizz, also nonalcoholic, juice 5 strawberries, 5 raspberries 1 apple, 1 stick celery, and 2 sprigs mint. Pour the juice into a soda syphon and add 2 measures cranberry juice. Add carbon dioxide, following the manufacturer's directions. Chill the charged vessel in the refrigerator for 1 hour, then pour the cocktail into a flute glass, garnish with ½ a strawberry, and serve.

caprissima da uva

½ **lime**, plus a wheel
  for decorating
5 **red grapes**, plus extra
  for decorating
2 measures **amber rum**
2 teaspoons **sugar**
2 teaspoons **velvet falernum**
crushed ice

Muddle the lime and grapes at the bottom of a glass.

Add the rum, sugar, and velvet falernum and fill the glass halfway with crushed ice. Churn the mixture with a muddler until thoroughly mixed.

Top the glass with more crushed ice, garnish with a lime wheel and grape, and serve.

For a Caprissima da Framoesa, muddle ½ lime, 5 raspberries, and 1 teaspoon pastis in a collins glass. Add 2 measures amber rum, 2 pink grapefruit slices, 2 teaspoons raspberry liqueur, 1 tablespoon sugar syrup, and fill the glass halfway with crushed ice. Churn with a muddler until thoroughly mixed. Top the glass with more crushed ice, garnish with a raspberry and a pink grapefruit wedge, and serve.

duke's daiquiri

makes **1**
glass **hurricane**
equipment **food processor
  or blender**

2 measures **white rum**
1 tablespoon **lime juice**
1 measure **sugar syrup**
tinned peach half, drained
1 measures **apple cider**
1 teaspoon **grenadine**
1 cup **ice cubes**

To garnish
lime wheel
black cherry

Add all ingredients to a food processor or blender and blend until smooth.

Pour into a glass, garnish with a lime wheel and a cherry, and serve.

For a Tahitian Pearl, add 2 measures 100 percent agave blanco tequila, 1 measure lime juice, 4 teaspoons agave syrup, 1 canned peach half, drained, 2 measures apple cider, 2 measures pineapple juice, 1 teaspoon grenadine, 5 mint leaves, and 1 cup of ice cubes to a food processor or blender and blend until smooth. Pour into a hurricane glass, garnish with a lime wheel and a basil leaf, and serve.

red rum

makes **2**
glasses **martini**
equipment **cocktail shaker,
   muddler, strainer**

handful of **red currants** or
   raspberries, plus extra t
   o garnish
1 measure **sloe gin**
4 measures **Bacardi
   8-year-old rum**
1 measure **lemon juice**
1 measure **vanilla syrup**
ice cubes

Muddle the red currants or raspberries and sloe gin
together in a cocktail shaker.

Add the rum, lemon juice, vanilla syrup, and some
ice cubes.

Shake and double-strain into 2 chilled martini glasses,
garnish with red currants or raspberries, and serve.

For a Rude Jude, put 2 measures white rum, a
generous dash each of strawberry syrup, strawberry
puree, and lime juice into a cocktail shaker with plenty
of ice. Shake and strain into 2 chilled martini glasses.

orange blossom

makes **2**
glasses **highball**
equipment **muddler, straws**

8 **orange slices**, plus wedges
   to garnish
4 teaspoons **almond syrup**
crushed ice
4 measures **pink grapefruit**
   juice
6 dashes **Angostura bitters**

Muddle half the orange slices and almond syrup in each glass. Fill the glasses with crushed ice and pour in the gin.

Stir, top up with the grapefruit juice and bitters, and garnish with orange wedges. Serve with straws.

For The Fix, mix 4 measures gin, 1 dash lime juice, 1 dash lemon juice, 1 dash pineapple juice, and 1 measure Cointreau in a cocktail shaker filled with ice. Shake and strain into 2 chilled highball glasses.

peach smash

makes **2**

glasses **old-fashioned**

equipment **cocktail shaker, muddler, strainer**

12 **mint leaves**, plus sprigs to garnish

6 **peach slices**

6 **lemon slices**, plus extra to garnish

4 teaspoons **superfine sugar**

4 measures **bourbon**

ice cubes, plus **cracked ice** to serve

Muddle the mint leaves, peach and lemon slices, and sugar in a cocktail shaker.

Add the bourbon and some ice cubes and shake well. Strain over cracked ice into 2 glasses. Garnish each with a mint sprig and a lemon slice and serve.

For a Rhett Butler, fill a cocktail shaker halfway with ice cubes, add 4 measures bourbon, 8 measures cranberry juice, 1/4 cup sugar syrup, and 2 tablespoons lime juice and shake well. Strain into 2 old-fashioned glasses filled with ice.

punches & sharers

white sangria

makes **1 large pitcher**

ice cubes
4 measures **vodka**
6 measures **apple juice**
2 measures **lemon juice**
2 measures **elderflower syrup**
6 measures **white wine**
6 measures **club soda**

To garnish
apple slices
lemon slices
mint leaves

Fill a pitcher with ice cubes, add all the remaining ingredients, and stir.

Garnish with apple and lemon slices and mint leaves and serve.

For Sakura Sangria, fill a large pitcher with ice cubes and add 4 measures cucumber-infused vodka (see page 12), 1½ measures elderflower syrup, 1 measure lemon juice, 1 measure umeshu, 4 measures apple juice, and 1 cup sparkling wine, then stir. Garnish with apple slices and cucumber strips and serve.

langra & tonic

makes **1 large pitcher**

ice cubes
1 cup **gin**
4 measures **mango juice**
2 measures **lemon juice**
2 measures **sugar**
1 cup **tonic water**
lemon wheels, to garnish

Fill a pitcher with ice cubes, add all the remaining ingredients, and stir. Garnish with lemon wheels and serve.

For Ginger Langra, add 4 measures ginger & green cardamom-infused gin (see page 13), 4 measures fino sherry, 2 measures sugar syrup, 2 measures mango juice, 2 measures lemon juice, and 1 cup tonic water to a large pitcher full of ice cubes and stir. Garnish with lime wheels and serve.

tinto de venezia

makes **1 large pitcher**

ice cubes
4 measures **Aperol**
4 measures **pink grapefruit juice**
4 measures **orange juice**
1 cup **rose wine**
4 measures **club soda**

To garnish
orange slices
grapefruit slices

Fill a pitcher with ice cubes. Add all the remaining ingredients and stir.

Garnish with orange and grapefruit slices and serve.

For a Vespertilio, add 4 measures raspberry-infused Aperol (see page 13), 4 measures pink grapefruit juice, 1 measure passion fruit syrup, the pulp of 2 passion fruit, and 1 ¼ cups chilled prosecco to a large pitcher full of ice cubes, stir, and serve.

lola's punch

makes **1 large pitcher**

ice cubes
4 measures **white rum**
3 measures **lemon juice**
3 measures **sugar syrup**
3 measures **apple juice**
3 measures **mango juice**
1 cup **white wine**
1 cup **club soda**

To garnish
mango slices
apple slices

Fill a pitcher with ice cubes, add all the remaining ingredient, and stir.

Garnish with mango and apple slices and serve.

For Colonial Punch, add 1 cup pineapple & cherry-infused white rum (see page 13), 2 measures lemon juice, 2 measures sugar syrup, 4 measures pineapple juice, and 1 cupsparkling wine to a large pitcher full of ice cubes and stir. Garnish with pineapple wedges and serve.

earl's punch

makes **1 pitcher**

ice cubes
4 measures **gin**
6 measures **Earl Grey tea**
6 measures pink **grapefruit juice**
6 measures **club soda**
1 measure **sugar syrup**

To garnish
pink grapefruit slices
black cherries

Fill a pitcher with ice cubes. Add all the remaining ingredients and stir.

Garnish with pink grapefruit slices and maraschino cherries and serve.

For Sylvestre Punch, put 4 measures gin, 1 tablespoon marmalade, 1 measure lemon juice, 4 measures orange juice, 4 measures pink grapefruit juice, 1 cup Earl Grey tea, and 6 measures mineral water into a food processor to blender and blend until smooth. Put in a soda syphon and charge with carbon dioxide, following the manufacturer's directions. Chill in the refrigerator for at least 1 hour in the soda syphon. Pour into a large serving bottle to serve.

mulled orchard

makes **1 large teapot**

1 pat **butter**
4 measures **apple juice**
1 measure **lemon juice**
1 measure **spiced sugar
  syrup** (see page 10)
4 measures **bourbon**
6 measures **hard apple cider**
cinnamon sticks, to garnish

Melt the butter in a saucepan over gentle heat.

Add the apple juice, lemon juice, spiced sugar syrup,
bourbon, and cider. Stir and heat until hot.

Pour carefully into a teapot and serve in heatproof
glasses, garnished with cinnamon sticks.

For Southern Belle, fill a large pitcher with ice cubes.
Add 6 measures bourbon, 2 measures lemon juice,
2 measures sugar syrup, 4 measures yellow tea,
2 measures apple juice, and 1 cup hard apple cider and
stir. Garnish with apple and lemon slices and serve.

pina coco

serves **2**

equipment **food processor, straws**

1 **pineapple**
4 measures **amber rum**
1 measure **Galliano**
1 measure **cream of coconut**
4 measures **passion fruit juice**
1 **banana**
1 cup **ice**

Cut the top off the pineapple and use a pineapple corer to remove the flesh inside the pineapple. Set aside the hollowed-out pineapple.

Cut the pineapple flesh into chunks. Add 7 chunks of the pineapple and the remaining ingredients to a food processor or blender and blend until smooth. Pour into the hollowed-out pineapple and serve with straws.

For rum punch, fill a large pitcher with ice cubes. Add 1 cup spiced rum, 4 measures lime juice, 4 measures sugar syrup, 6 measures passion fruit juice, 6 measures pineapple juice, and 6 measures orange juice and stir. Garnish with orange and lime slices and passion fruit halves and serve.

la rochelle punch

makes **1 large pitcher**

4 measures **Cognac**
½ cup **frozen mixed berries**,
   plus extra to serve
ice cubes
4 measures **apple juice**
2 measures **lemon juice**
2 measures **sugar syrup**
1¼ cups **ginger ale**

Add the Cognac and berries to a food processor or blender and blend until smooth. Pour into a pitcher. Add plenty of ice cubes and the remaining ingredients to the pitcher and stir. Garnish with berries and serve.

For Spice Route Punch, add 1 cup ginger-infused Cognac (see page 12) and ½ cup frozen mixed berries to a food processor or blender and blend until smooth. Pour into a pitcher full of ice cubes, add 1 measure cinnamon syrup, 1 cup apple cider, 2 measures lemon juice, 1 measure sugar syrup, and 1 cup club soda and stir. Garnish with cinnamon sticks and apple slices and serve.

blue grass punch

makes **1 large pitcher**

4 measures **bourbon**
1 tablespoon **marmalade**
2 measures **lemon juice**
1 measure **sugar syrup**
2 measures **cranberry juice**
6 measures **club soda**
ice cubes
dried orange wheels,
   to garnish

Add the bourbon and marmalade to a pitcher and stir until dissolved.

Add all the remaining ingredients and fill the pitcher with ice cubes. Stir.

Garnish with dried orange wheels and serve.

For Baton Blanc, put 4 measures bourbon, 2 measures lemon juice, 2 measures orange juice, 2 measures sugar syrup, and 2 teaspoons marmalade into a food processor or blender and blend until smooth. Pour into a large pitcher, add 1 cup wheat beer, and fill the pitcher with ice cubes. Garnish with orange wheels and serve.

watermelon punch

serves 2
equipment **food processor, straws**

1 small **watermelon**
1 cup **vodka**
20 **mint leaves**
3 measures **lemon**
5 measures **sugar syrup**
1 cup **ice cubes**
lemon wheels, to garnish

Cut the top off the watermelon and use a spoon to scoop out the flesh inside. Set aside the hollowed-out watermelon.

Remove the seeds from the watermelon flesh, then add the flesh and the remaining ingredients to a food processor or blender and blend until smooth. Pour into the hollowed-out watermelon, garnish with lemon wheels, and serve with straws

For Afternoon Watermelon, to serve 6, add 1 cup watermelon juice, 10 strawberries, hulled, and 5 mint leaves to a food processor or blender and process until smooth. Strain and then pour into a 1-liter swing-top bottle. Add 1 cup mint-infused vodka (see page 13), 1 measure elderflower syrup, 1 tablespoon lemon juice, and 2 cups club soda and stir. Chill in the refrigerator for at least 2 hours before serving.

blush sangria

makes **1 large pitcher**

4 measures **vodka**

2 measures **crème de framboise**

1 cup **rose wine**

6 measures **cranberry juice**

2 measures **lime juice**

1 measure **sugar syrup**

6 measures **club soda**

ice cubes

edible flower petals, to garnish

Add all ingredients to a pitcher, then fill the pitcher with ice cubes.

Stir and garnish with edible flowers.

For Sakura Punch, fill a large pitcher with ice cubes. Add 4 measures vodka, 1 cup rose wine, 4 measures lychee juice, 4 measures pink grapefruit juice, 1 measure rose syrup (see page 9), 1 measure lemon juice, and 6 measures club soda and stir. Garnish with canned lychees, lemon slices, and maraschino cherries and serve.

torino spritzer

makes **1 large pitcher**

ice cubes
4 measures **sweet vermouth**
4 measures **Campari**
4 measures **Triple Sec**
4 measures **lemon juice**
1 cup **lemon-lime soda**
1 cup **red wine**

To garnish
lemon slices
orange slices
grapefruit slices

Fill a pitcher with ice cubes. Add all the remaining ingredients to a pitcher and stir.

Garnish with lemon, orange, and grapefruit slices and serve.

For Gaseosa Tinto, add 4 measures sweet vermouth, 4 measures dry vermouth, 4 measures Campari, 2 measures orange & fennel seed shrub (see page 11), 2 measures lemon juice, 4 measures red wine, and 1 cup club soda to a large pitcher with ice cubes and stir. Garnish with an orange wheels and serve.

pimm's cocktail

makes **2**
glasses **highball**
equipment **muddler**

ice cubes
2 measures **Pimm's No. 1**
2 measures **gin**
4 measures **lemon-lime soda**
4 measures **ginger ale**

To garnish
cucumber strips
blueberries
orange slices

Fill 2 highball glasses with ice cubes. Add the remaining ingredients, one by one in order, over the ice. Garnish with cucumber strips, blueberries, and orange slices and serve.

For an On the Lawn, fill 2 highball glasses with ice and fresh fruit such as strawberries and oranges. Add 2 measures Pimm's No. 1 and 2 measures gin to each one and top up with lemon-lime soda and ginger ale.

planter's punch

makes **2**
glasses **highball**
equipment **cocktail shaker,
strainer**

4 measures **Myer's Jamaican
Planter's Punch rum**
8 drops **Angostura bitters**
1 measure **lime juice**
4 measures **chilled water**
2 measures **sugar syrup**
ice cubes

To garnish
orange slices
lime slices

Put the rum, bitters, lime juice, water, and sugar syrup into a cocktail shaker and add some ice cubes.

Shake and strain into 2 chilled glasses. Garnish with orange and lime slices and serve.

For a Tempo, put 3 ice cubes, cracked, into each of 2 chilled highball glasses and pour 1 measure white rum, 1 measure lime juice, and ½ measure crème de cacao into each glass. Add a dash of Angostura bitters, stir, and top up with lemon-lime soda. Garnish with lime slices and serve.

garden cooler

makes **1 punch bowl**, about
  5 litres (10 pints)

3 cups **London dry gin**
2 cups **lemon juice**
1 cup **sugar syrup**
1 cup **elderflower syrup**
2 cups **green tea**
2 cups **mint tea**
2 cups **apple juice**
2 cups **club soda**
ice cubes
peach slices, to garnish

Add all the ingredients to a punch bowl and stir.

Garnish with peach slices and serve.

For English Garden Fizz, add 2 cups London dry gin and 1 bunch mint leaves to a large punch bowl and steep for 1 hour. Remove the mint, add 1 cup Triple Sec, 1 cup lemon juice, 1 cup sugar syrup, 1 cup cucumber juice, 1 cup apple juice, 2 cups green tea, 2 cups club soda, and some ice cubes to the punch bowl and stir. Garnish with cucumber slices and serve.

index

acknowledgments

Commissioning Editor: Eleanor Maxfield
Editor: Pauline Bache
Designer: Geoff Fennell
Special Photography: Jonathan Kennedy
Special Recipes and Styling: Tom Soden & Felix von Nida
Picture Library Manager: Jennifer Veall
Production Controller: Sarah Kramer

Special Photography © Octopus Publishing Group Limited/Jonathan Kennedy: Additional photography © Octopus Publishing Group Limited/Stephen Conroy